100 QUESTIONS

about

WOMEN WHO DARED!

and all
the answers
too!

Written and Illustrated by
Simon Abbott

PETER PAUPER PRESS, INC.
White Plains, New York

For Sally - keep daring!

PETER PAUPER PRESS

In 1928, at the age of twenty-two, Peter Beilenson began printing books on a small press in the basement of his parents' home in Larchmont, New York. Peter—and later, his wife, Edna—sought to create fine books that sold at "prices even a pauper could afford."

Today, still family owned and operated, Peter Pauper Press continues to honor our founders' legacy of quality, value, and fun for big kids and small kids alike.

Designed by Heather Zschock

Text and illustrations copyright © 2021 by Simon Abbott

Published by Peter Pauper Press, Inc.
202 Mamaroneck Avenue
White Plains, New York 10601 USA

Published in the United Kingdom and Europe by Peter Pauper Press, Inc.
c/o White Pebble International
Unit 2, Plot 11 Terminus Rd.
Chichester, West Sussex PO19 8TX, UK

Library of Congress Cataloging-in-Publication Data Available

ISBN 978-1-4413-3697-2
Manufactured for Peter Pauper Press, Inc.
Printed in China

7 6 5 4 3 2 1

Visit us at www.peterpauper.com

Welcome to the wonderful world
of amazing women.

You'll meet sports stars with jam-packed trophy cabinets,
scientists making medical discoveries, and activists who
changed the course of history.

**Which mathematician helped humankind
reach the moon?**

Who was the first fearless female explorer
to sail around the world?

**How did a group of clever codebreakers
help to end WWII?**

All these questions, and many more, will be answered
as we turn the page and introduce ourselves
to the Women Who Dared!

HOW
DARE
YOU!

USE YOUR IMAGINATION!

Let's start with a collection of creative women, whose talent has brought joy to our lives!

Who's first on the list?

Maya Angelou was a phenomenal woman. She's best known as the author of over 30 books, and wrote about the story of her childhood in *I Know Why the Caged Bird Sings*. This autobiography has sold over a million copies even though it's one of the most frequently-banned books in the USA. Maya was also a dancer, singer, actor, director, and worked alongside Dr. Martin Luther King, Jr. as a civil rights campaigner in the 1960s. In 1993, she read her poem "On the Pulse of Morning" at President Bill Clinton's inauguration.

Have any other women made their mark with poetry?

Sappho lived over 2,600 years ago on the island of Lesbos in Greece. In ancient times, she was known simply as "the poetess," and her talent was celebrated with coins and statues. Sappho is famous for her poems about love and emotion, many of which could be sung accompanied by a musical instrument called a lyre.

Let's keep flicking through the history books!
Who's a story-telling superstar?
Murasaki Shikibu wrote *The Tale of Genji*, which is considered the first novel
in the history of the world! She lived over 1,000 years ago, and worked as a tutor
to Empress Shoshi at the Imperial Court in Japan. Murasaki's trailblazing tale is
made up of 54 separate books and 795 different poems. Happy reading!

Who is famous for adventure stories or spooky tales?
In 1816, **Mary Shelley** was on vacation with a group of young writers who decided
to have a competition telling horror stories. Mary couldn't think of one at first. That
night, she had a nightmare, wrote the tale down, and had the book published. Its
title was *Frankenstein*, and it was the world's first science fiction novel. It tells the
story of a smart scientist called Victor Frankenstein, who brings a strange creature
to life. This "man-monster" turns out to be a frightful character, who is rejected by
Victor and the rest of society. The monster goes on to seek his revenge! Scary stuff!

Art museums are full of historic paintings by men. Did any women become famous painters back in the day?

Back in the 17th century, many people thought that women were too "delicate" to work in the male-dominated art world, and talented women were denied chances to shine. But brilliant Italian artist Artemisia Gentileschi proved the naysayers wrong. She worked throughout Europe for clients including the King of Spain and the Grand Duke of Tuscany. She once painted a picture of herself at work: *Self-Portrait as the Allegory of Painting*. Take a look on the right—do you think you could paint a self-portrait standing in that position?

What about a more modern female artist who made her mark?

Frida Kahlo was a Mexican artist whose work hugely influenced the art world. She trained to become a doctor, but a terrible car accident ended her studies. It took months to recover, so Frida started painting to take her mind off her discomfort and boredom. She often explored the theme of pain in her colorful works. She was a confident artist, who painted over 55 bold self-portraits to express her feelings and experiences. Kahlo was incredibly proud of her Mexican heritage, and her bright, symbolic paintings are full of flowers, feathers, dancing, music, animals, and patterns.

Who wowed the world with her extraordinary photo skills?

Lee Miller, a pioneering photographer, was just one of four female photojournalists allowed to travel with the U.S. Armed Forces in World War II. She wore a custom-made steel helmet designed to accommodate her camera. Being on the front line put Lee in great danger, and her photos of the inhumane conditions at German concentration camps shocked the world. She accompanied newly-freed prisoners to the hospital and joined in their celebrations of freedom. A former inmate of one concentration camp called Dachau recalled, "She was the only one of the liberators that stayed with us."

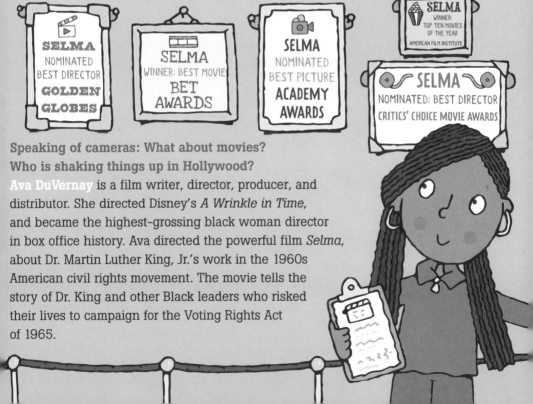

SELMA
NOMINATED
BEST DIRECTOR
GOLDEN GLOBES

SELMA
WINNER: BEST MOVIE
BET AWARDS

SELMA
NOMINATED
BEST PICTURE
ACADEMY AWARDS

SELMA
WINNER:
TOP TEN MOVIES
OF THE YEAR
AMERICAN FILM INSTITUTE

SELMA
NOMINATED: BEST DIRECTOR
CRITICS' CHOICE MOVIE AWARDS

Speaking of cameras: What about movies?
Who is shaking things up in Hollywood?

Ava DuVernay is a film writer, director, producer, and distributor. She directed Disney's *A Wrinkle in Time*, and became the highest-grossing black woman director in box office history. Ava directed the powerful film *Selma*, about Dr. Martin Luther King, Jr.'s work in the 1960s American civil rights movement. The movie tells the story of Dr. King and other Black leaders who risked their lives to campaign for the Voting Rights Act of 1965.

Have any women struck a note in the world of classical music?

Clara Schumann was born over 200 years ago, and left a huge impression on musical history. As a child, she received daily lessons in piano, violin, singing, music theory, harmony, and composition. She composed 23 musical pieces, and performed in concert tours throughout Europe for 61 years. Clara was one of the first pianists to play from memory. Unusually for the time, she was the main breadwinner in the Schumann household.

Not all performers can be treated to daily music lessons. Which singer overcame challenging circumstances to succeed in the world's spotlight?

Ella Fitzgerald survived the deaths of her parents and a miserable time at a reform school to become the "First Lady of Song." Her extraordinary jazz vocals won her 13 Grammy awards and over 40 million album sales. Despite her talent and early success, Ella continued to suffer discrimination from music venues, but then along came Marilyn Monroe. The world-famous actress was a huge fan of Ella's, and had reportedly learned to sing by listening to Fitzgerald's records. Monroe called a nightclub owner and told him that if he booked Ella, she promised to sit at the front table every single night. The newspapers went wild, and Ella never had to play a small club again!

Who else's musical success had a shaky start?

Record-breaking musical star **Gloria Estefan** was born in Cuba, but was forced to flee to Miami, Florida following Fidel Castro's coup in 1959. Thirty-one years later, the singer was seriously injured in a bus crash, which left her with a broken back. She made her comeback with a brand-new album and world tour, so to add to her triumphs, Gloria wins the "Superstar Survivor" prize. In fact, Gloria's achievements could fill this whole book. She has sold over 100 million records, had 38 Billboard number 1 hits, and won 7 Grammy awards. She earned the Presidential Medal of Freedom and a Kennedy Center Honor, too! She's a singer, songwriter, actress, author, businesswoman, and philanthropist. *¡Felicidades!*

We've had musicians and singers. Who's a contender for the "Dance Diva" award?

My vote goes to **Misty Copeland**. Three months after taking her first ballet class, 13-year-old Misty was dancing en pointe (which means dancing on the tips of your toes). In just over a year, she was performing professionally—an achievement that takes most dancers many years of study.

In 2015, Misty won the role of principal dancer at the American Ballet Theater, the first Black woman to hold that position in the company's 75-year history. Go Misty!

9

WE CAN WORK IT OUT!

It's time to turn our attention to the scientists who smashed the glass ceiling, and the mathematicians who had it all worked out!

Which scientist was a groundbreaking myth-buster?

Until the natural scientist Maria Sibylla Merian came along, most people believed that insects simply materialized from mud! Maria's detailed illustrations in the 17th century led to brand-new discoveries about plants and insects. Famous naturalist David Attenborough considers her one of the most important contributors to the study of insects.

Who else was a natural science pioneer?

Let's hear it for Mary Anning, a she-ro of fossil discovery. Like many poor girls growing up in the 1800s, she had little education, but taught herself to read and write. Most of her days were spent with her brother on the U.K.'s Dorset beaches, searching for items to sell. One day, 12-year-old Mary uncovered what she thought was a crocodile skull. In fact, it was the fossil of a prehistoric reptile called an ichthyosaur *(IK-thee-uh-sawr)*. She continued to explore Dorset's Jurassic Coast, and in her lifetime discovered the skeleton of a long-necked plesiosaur *(PLES-io-sawr)* and a flying dimorphodon *(di-MOR-foe-don)*. Mary was forced to sell many of her fossils to male scientists in order to pay off the family debts. These men would rarely credit her in the scientific papers they wrote, and despite her achievements, the Geographical Society of London refused to admit Mary as a member. Mary Anning's legacy as one of the greatest fossil-hunters of all time is celebrated at London's Natural History Museum, where many of her sensational finds are on display today.

Which sea-based scientist made a splash in the ocean?

Have you heard of "The Shark Lady"? As a young girl, Eugenie Clark developed a fascination for sea creatures when she spent hours each weekend at the New York Aquarium. As a fish biologist, or ichthyologist *(IK-thee-o-lo-jist)*, she dove beneath the sea countless times to get up close with marine life, particularly sharks. She discovered a fish species called the Moses sole, which has a natural shark repellent, making a hungry shark screech to a halt and thrash its head about. This daring woman even rode on the back of a 50-foot (15 m) whale shark, and took her last dive at 92 years old!

That takes some nerve! Were any other scientists playing with fire?

Katia Krafft, along with her husband Maurice, were leading volcanologists.

Hold on! What's a volcanologist?

It's a super-smart scientist who studies the creation and eruption of volcanoes. The Kraffts were often first on the scene to any volcanic blow-up, and they filmed and photographed eruptions up close. In 1991, they used their footage of the 1985 eruption of the Nevado del Ruiz volcano to convince the Philippine president to evacuate the area around her own erupting volcano, Mount Pinatubo. This saved hundreds if not thousands of lives. The Kraffts were fearless, and would often work within a few feet of a super-hot lava flow. Sadly, their bravery cost them their lives, and they were engulfed by a lava flow during a 1991 research trip to Mt. Unzen in Japan.

How long have women been involved in mathematics?

A long time! **Hypatia** is the first female mathematician whose life we know about. She lived in Alexandria, Egypt, around 1,600 years ago. Hypatia was brought up by her father, Theon, who rejected the traditional role given to a daughter and raised her like a son. Hypatia grew up learning math, astronomy, and philosophy. Wearing the male-only robes of the academic elite, she went on to teach students who traveled great distances to hear her lectures.

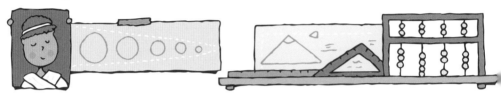

Did any female mathematicians start out in a totally different career?

Maria Gaetana Agnesi was born in Italy over 300 years ago. She had set her heart on becoming a nun, but her father begged her to change her mind. She agreed on three conditions:

1. She could go to church whenever she wanted.
2. She could dress in simple clothes.
3. She could stop taking trips to theaters, dances, and other entertainments.

This meant that Maria had oodles of free time to study religion and mathematics, as well as educate her 21 brothers and sisters. Her research paid off. She became the first woman to write a math handbook, and to be appointed a mathematics professor!

Who was the world's first computer programmer?

Ada Lovelace was a 19th-century math genius. Unusually for the time, her mother made sure that young Ada was taught logic, science, and math, and encouraged her obsession with machines. In 1833, Ada befriended the inventor Charles Babbage, and became fascinated with his plans for a computer prototype called the Analytical Engine. Lovelace jotted down her suggestions for how the machine could work, and what codes it could use. These notes have been described as early computer programs, and inspired Alan Turing's work on the first modern computer over 100 years later!

We often hear about "putting a man on the Moon."
Who were the women who launched humankind into space?
On February 20th, 1962, astronaut John Glenn became the first American to orbit Earth. He had refused to take off until the space flight calculations were verified by one woman: Katherine Johnson. Johnson was captivated by numbers from a young age, and began counting the steps to church, or the dishes she had washed. After becoming a teacher and mom, Johnson joined NASA in 1953, with the job title "computer"! Upon her death at 101, NASA Administrator Jim Bridenstine paid tribute to her:

> "Her dedication and skill as a mathematician helped put humans on the Moon and before that made it possible for our astronauts to take the first steps in space that we now follow on a journey to Mars."

Who else deserves a space race shout-out?

In 1969, Margaret Hamilton's groundbreaking work for Apollo 11's rocketship flight software helped to land the first humans on the Moon. The landing was hazardous. Minutes before the lunar lander reached the surface of the Moon, several computer alarms were activated. NASA had to decide whether to abort the mission or keep going. Thanks to the precautions that Hamilton had put in place, the NASA team could see that the alarms weren't significant, and the landing was a success. Phew!

Let's pay a visit to the engineering hall of fame!
Which innovator deserves a gold star?
Born in 1909, Beatrix "Tilly" Shilling spent her childhood pocket money on "Meccano" construction toys, penknives, a monkey wrench, glue, and a tool box. After studying engineering at Manchester University, Tilly took up motorcycle racing, and fitted her bike with a state-of-the-art supercharger which allowed her to race at speeds of 106 mph (171 km/h). World War II was on the horizon, and Tilly was given a tough problem to solve. The Royal Air Force's Hurricane and Spitfires would cut out when the planes went into a steep dive. This put the pilots in great danger. Tilly invented a device which stopped the surge of fuel, and in doing so, helped to win WWII!

Who else changed the course of modern warfare?
"The brains of people are more interesting than the looks, I think." That's a quote from Hollywood actress Hedy Lamarr, who began her film career in the 1930s. At the beginning of WWII, Lamarr and the composer George Antheil created a radio guidance system for torpedoes that enabled them to "hop" from one frequency to another, making them undetectable to the enemy. This technology was adopted by the U.S. Navy in 1957, and elements of their invention can be found in Bluetooth and Wi-Fi technology today.

What other female engineer's work is still in use today?
The Brooklyn Bridge, among other things! The contract was awarded to civil engineer John Roebling, assisted by his son Washington Roebling. Sadly, John died in an accident while he was searching for potential bridge locations. Then Washington became desperately ill, and could only observe the bridge from a telescope in bed. His wife, **Emily Warren Roebling**, came to the rescue. She communicated with the engineers, negotiated contracts, and solved baffling engineering puzzles. In 1883, after 14 years of construction, the Brooklyn Bridge was finished! Everyone agreed that the first rider across the bridge should be Emily, who sat in her carriage with a rooster on her lap as the workers took off their hats and cheered her on!

Who made the medical field much healthier?
Born 200 years ago, **Florence Nightingale** came from a wealthy family. She turned down a marriage proposal, and instead enrolled as a nursing student. During the Crimean War (1853–1856), the British government asked her to organize a group of 34 nurses to look after wounded soldiers. Nothing prepared Nightingale for the horrendous conditions. The base hospital was disgusting, rats and bugs scuttled about, they didn't have necessary supplies, water was rationed, and more soldiers died of diseases than battle injuries. Nightingale cleaned up the hospital, established a laundry, kitchen, classroom, and library, then wrote an 830-page report on how to operate future military hospitals. After 18 months, she returned home to a hero's welcome. The government granted her a prize of $250,000, which she used to create St. Thomas' Hospital and The Nightingale Training School for Nurses.

Did any other women play an important role in the Crimean War?
Jamaican-born **Mary Seacole** was introduced to nursing at a young age, and cared for the victims of Kingston's cholera epidemic in the 1850s. At the outbreak of the Crimean War, Mary traveled to England and asked the War Office to send her to Crimea to look after the wounded soldiers. They refused. Undeterred, Mary paid for her own passage to the battlefronts, where she set up the British Hotel to care for the sick and injured. She bravely visited the battlefield, sometimes dodging gunfire, to nurse the wounded soldiers. Her kindness earned her the name "Mother Seacole."

Who else was shaking up the medical field in the mid-1800s?

In 1849, **Elizabeth Blackwell** became the first woman to receive a medical degree in the United States. She was determined to train as a physician after a dying friend told her that she would have been spared some pain if her doctor had been a woman. Blackwell helped to open the New York Infirmary for Women and Children in 1857. In Britain, she founded the National Health Society, with its slogan "Prevention is Better than Cure." Wise words indeed!

Whose medical achievements have been a little overlooked?

In the early 1900s, leprosy was rife in Hawaii. Step forward, **Alice Ball**. She was the first woman and the first Black American to earn a master's degree in chemistry from the College of Hawaii. She found a way to make a water-soluble solution from the oil of the chaulmoogra tree, which could be injected to effectively treat leprosy patients with minimal side-effects. This treatment was used for the next 20 years until a full cure was discovered.

Why haven't we heard of her?

Arthur Dean, the President of the University of Hawaii, took her research as his own and called the treatment "the Dean method." In his scientific paper, Alice Ball wasn't even mentioned.

Who else's breakthrough was written out of scientific history?

Pretty much all living things are what they are because of DNA: molecules full of information about how each living thing will look and function. **Rosalind Franklin** was a scientist who specialized in X-ray photography. In May 1952, she took an image, called Photograph 51, which captured the pattern of DNA. This would help scientists understand this molecule's structure. Without her knowledge, her colleague Maurice Wilkins showed the image to James Watson, who, with Francis Crick, published a paper on DNA's structure, and went on to win the 1963 Nobel Prize for Physiology and Medicine. They used Rosalind's photograph as evidence, but never credited her with this landmark discovery.

ATHLETES AND ADVENTURERS

Let's catch up with some sports superheroines! On your mark. . . get set. . . go!

Which sports superstar was an early achiever?
Simone Biles, one of the greatest gymnasts of all time, got her start at just 6 years old. On a field trip to a gymnastics studio, little Simone watched and copied the gymnasts' moves, launching her athletic career. To date, her talent and dedication have won Biles over 25 World Championship medals. She never fails to wow her audience (and the judges) with her gravity-defying moves, many of which have never been seen before in a gymnastics competition. Check out her double-double dismount from the beam, or her triple-double on the floor!

What about record-breaking women in the world of figure skating?
Retired figure skater Yuna Kim was the first sportswoman to win all four of the world's biggest figure skating competitions. She was no stranger to the winner's podium, as she took first, second, or third in every single figure skating competition she entered. Kim began skating at 6 years old, became the first South Korean figure skater to win a medal at the 2010 Olympic Games, and dazzled her fans with her speed, style, and her triple-triple jumps!

Does sporting super-stardom ever run in the family?

Let's hear it for the incomparable tennis greats: the Williams sisters. Between them, Venus and Serena Williams have clocked up an incredible 122 singles titles (49 for Venus, 73 for Serena). Serena's fastest serve was recorded at the 2013 Australian Open, where she clocked an incredible 128 mph (206 km/h). That's faster than a tornado!

Have the Williams sisters ever played together?

Venus and Serena formed an awesome doubles partnership, as you can imagine! Their trophy cabinet is stuffed with 14 grand slam doubles titles and 3 Olympic gold medals.

Have any women with disabilities rocketed to sports stardom?

Three cheers for the swimming sensation, Trischa Zorn! She's the most successful athlete in the history of the Paralympic Games, having won an incredible 55 medals in her career. Trischa was born blind, and began swimming at the age of 10. She went on to compete in seven Paralympic Games, and topped the individual medals table at the 1992 Barcelona Games.

Whose sports skills led her to some out-of-this-world places?
Valentina Tereshkova's skydiving skill helped earn her a place in the Russian
space program, and she became the first woman to travel in space. She took a
70.8-hour flight aboard the Vostok 6 spacecraft in 1963, and orbited Earth 48
times. The launch and flight were successful, and on her descent Valentina ejected
from the space capsule four miles above Earth. Although she encountered strong
winds, Valentina landed her parachute safely, with just a bruise on her nose
to show for her adventure!

Have any athletes made history in the sea?
The 21-mile (34 km) stretch of sea between England and France, called the
English Channel, has always been seen as a unique sporting challenge.
Swimmers battle wind, cold temperatures, high waves, and the odd jellyfish!
In 1926, Olympic gold medalist **Gertrude Ederele** became the first woman to
conquer this notorious trial. She battled stormy conditions, but completed the
swim in a record-breaking 14 hours and 31 minutes.

What about barriers to women becoming sports stars?
The Boston Marathon is the world's oldest annual marathon, having begun in 1897. Unbelievably, women were barred from entering the race for the first 74 years of its existence. In 1966, **Roberta Gibb** hid behind a bush at the start of the race and ran the marathon without an official number. The following year, **Katherine Switzer** applied, using her initials on the form instead of her name, and managed to enter the race officially. Organizers in charge of the race tried to physically remove her once they spotted her among the runners. Despite these attacks, Switzer completed the marathon in an impressive 4 hours and 20 minutes, making headlines the next day!

Who has rocked the world of rock climbing?
In 1994, Lynn Hill became the first person to free-climb the daunting 3,000-foot (914 m) "Nose" on El Capitan in Yosemite National Park within 24 hours. Free climbing is when someone uses their physical ability to climb a rock using footholds and handholds, just relying on ropes to prevent injury rather than to help with the climb itself. The sheer granite rock face of El Capitan has been described as "the world's hardest climb," with a challenging mix of steepness, slipperiness, and height. Hill's power, flexibility, and determination were the perfect combination when it came to her record-breaking rock climb.

21

Who was the first woman to travel all the way around the world, and how did she do it?

In her search for new types of plants, the botanist Jeanne Baret became the first woman to circumnavigate the world in 1766. At the time, the French navy had a rule banning women from their ships, so Jeanne had to dress as a man to set sail around the globe. Her disguise worked for more than two years. She collected over 6,000 plant specimens, including the bougainvillea, which she named after the ship's captain. Her cover was eventually blown, and the captain, Admiral Bougainvillea, had no choice but to leave her behind on Mauritius, a small island in the Indian Ocean. She remained on the island and opened a tavern before completing her circumnavigation of the world when she returned to France around 1775.

They say "the sky's the limit."
Was the sky not the limit for any daring women?

When Bessie Coleman's brothers returned from France after fighting in World War I, she was fascinated by their stories of French women who trained as pilots. Bessie was determined to fly. She applied to one U.S. flight school after another, but each time she was rejected because she was a Black woman. She didn't give up. She took French classes at night school, completed applications to flight schools in France, and finally received her pilot's license from the Fédération Aéronautique Internationale in 1921. The following year she performed the first public flight by a Black woman. Bessie toured the U.S. giving flight lessons and performing her famous "loop-the-loop" in air shows.

Why did the librarian get kicked off the plane?

'Coz it was overbooked!

Who else deserves a traveling trailblazer award?

Lady Hester Stanhope was born in 1776, at a time when wealthy women were discouraged from being too adventurous. Hester was intelligent, independent, and unafraid to voice her opinions. At 33 years old, she set off to travel the world, visiting Gibraltar, Malta, Greece, Egypt, Palestine, Lebanon, and Syria. Along the way, she lost all her fine clothes in a shipwreck, so Hester started dressing like the local Turkish men. She liked the look so much she kept on wearing it, and even carried a sword. She went on to lead some of the first archaeological digs in Palestine.

Which globetrotting woman liked a challenge?

Nellie Bly was a groundbreaking journalist, who was inspired after reading *Around the World in Eighty Days* by Jules Verne. She made it her mission to circumnavigate the globe in just 75 days, and revealed her plans to Joseph Pulitzer, her newspaper boss. He was less than encouraging, telling her that "no-one but a man can do this."

Did his prediction come true? What did she do?

Nellie traveled light. She wore one dress, and packed some underwear, toiletries, pens, a dressing gown, flask, cup, two caps, three veils, slippers, needle and thread, and some handkerchiefs. She smashed the world record by completing the adventure in just 72 days. She traveled by train, steamship, rickshaw, horse, and donkey. While in France, she even had time for a visit to Jules Verne himself!

IT'S BUSINESS TIME!

Let's knock on the boardroom door and say hello to the women who took the business world by storm!

What historic hurdles did women have to face as entrepreneurs?

High on the list were laws which, of course, were written by men. In England, married women weren't allowed to own property until 1882. In 1922, women were finally allowed to inherit money as men did. It wasn't until 1975 that women were allowed to open a bank account in their own name! In 1848, the Married Woman's Property Act passed in New York, allowing a woman to collect rents, receive an inheritance, file a lawsuit, and not be automatically liable for her husband's debts. All U.S. states passed their own versions of this law by 1900.

Which phenomenal woman persevered all the same?

Mary Katherine Goddard was described as "a woman of extraordinary judgment, energy, nerve, and strong good sense." In 1766, she became the first woman publisher in the United States, and in 1775 she became the country's first female postmaster, supervising mail delivery and managing her post office. She is famous for printing the very first copy of the Declaration of Independence, and was the only woman to sign it, too!

Which enterprising woman succeeded against all the odds?

Elizabeth Hobbs Keckley was born into slavery in 1818. She bought her and her son's freedom in 1855, and started a dressmaking business to support herself. Her skill and expertise impressed the First Lady, Mary Todd Lincoln. Keckley became her favorite seamstress, friend, and traveling companion. During her time at the White House, she founded a charity for people recently freed from slavery, which distributed clothes, food, and shelter to those in need.

Whose personal experience inspired her business empire?

Madam C.J. Walker was the first self-made millionaire in the United States. She was born on a cotton plantation in 1867, and, like many Black women of the time, suffered from brittle and patchy hair due to the harsh hair treatments that were available. She created her own hair care line, and traveled around the country to promote her products. By 1917, Madam C.J. Walker's company had trained nearly 20,000 women as sales agents, who went door-to-door selling pomades and shampoos. Much of the company's profits were donated to organizations to improve the lives of Black communities, and she founded the Lelia College to teach young women hairstyling skills. As she once said, "Don't sit down and wait for the opportunities to come. Get up and make them!"

Which determined woman built her business on word of mouth?

Estée Lauder was born in New York in 1906, the daughter of a Hungarian mother and Czech father. Her chemist uncle taught her how to create skin creams, and she began to sell her cosmetics to women under the dryers in hair salons. Her big break came when department store Saks Fifth Avenue placed an $800 order for her beauty creams. Lauder was a pioneer in sales and marketing techniques, but never forgot that women who liked her products would "spread the word." She became one of the richest self-made women in the world. As the lady herself once said, "I never dreamed about success. I worked for it!"

Which businesswoman was way ahead of the curve?

In 1976, Anita Roddick founded The Body Shop in a tiny, green-painted store in Brighton, U.K. Today the company's products are sold in 3,000 stores in over 70 countries. Roddick believed that her business could be a force for good. Her skincare products were sold in refillable bottles, and the ingredients were sustainably sourced and paid for fairly. Anita Roddick was an activist, and used her growing business as a platform to highlight the destruction of the Amazon Rainforest, and the use of sperm whale oil in the production of regular cosmetics. She fought against animal testing of beauty products from day one, and empowered women worldwide with her Community Fair Trade program.

Who could be described as the "First Lady of Finance"?

Muriel Siebert shattered the glass ceiling in 1967, when she became the first woman to own a seat on the New York Stock Exchange. Just 13 years earlier, she had driven 700 miles (1,127 km) from Cleveland to Manhattan in a used car with just $500 in savings. She had to get a job . . . and quick! She finally landed a position at the brokerage firm Bache & Co., and began to rise through the ranks when she used just the initial "M" on her applications, in place of "Muriel." She suffered many setbacks and rejections along the way, but her determination won the day and she took her historic seat at just 35 years old. It would take another 10 years before a second woman joined her.

Who made her mark on the world of media?

Arianna Huffington founded *The Huffington Post*, an online newspaper, in 2005. It quickly became one of the top news sites on the internet. Six years after its launch, AOL bought the company for $315 million. Arianna didn't put her feet up. She founded Thrive Global, an organization that aims to change the way we live and work, reducing stress and burn-out.

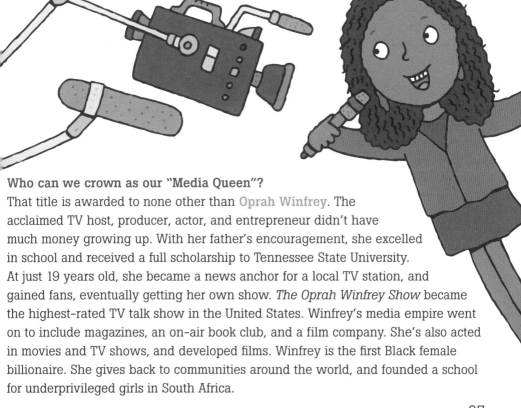

Who can we crown as our "Media Queen"?

That title is awarded to none other than Oprah Winfrey. The acclaimed TV host, producer, actor, and entrepreneur didn't have much money growing up. With her father's encouragement, she excelled in school and received a full scholarship to Tennessee State University. At just 19 years old, she became a news anchor for a local TV station, and gained fans, eventually getting her own show. *The Oprah Winfrey Show* became the highest-rated TV talk show in the United States. Winfrey's media empire went on to include magazines, an on-air book club, and a film company. She's also acted in movies and TV shows, and developed films. Winfrey is the first Black female billionaire. She gives back to communities around the world, and founded a school for underprivileged girls in South Africa.

WARRIORS AND WARTIME

It's time to take a look at fearless female fighters who have helped to change the course of history. Stand to attention!

Where do we start with our list of warrior women?

Let's travel back nearly 2,000 years to ancient Britain. The Romans are in charge, but they face an uprising from the rebel Iceni tribe. The tribe seeks revenge after the Romans stole land, property, and publicly flogged their queen, Boudica. She had trained as a warrior, and had been schooled in weaponry and fighting techniques. Boudica was determined to overthrow the Romans, and led her tribe into battle. She defeated the Romans' Ninth Legion and destroyed Camulodunum, the capital of Roman Britain. The Romans finally beat the rebels, but at a steep cost. Reports claim that although the rebellion failed, Boudica's forces finished off 70,000 Roman soldiers.

Were any other British queens famously fearsome?

In 1588, a fleet of Spanish ships were on their way to England to overthrow Queen Elizabeth I. An army of 4,000 English soldiers gathered to defend the mouth of the River Thames. The Queen, dressed in armor, traveled by horseback to review her troops and declared that she was "resolved, in the midst and heat of the battle, to live and die amongst you all; to lay down for my God, and for my kingdom, and my people, my honor and my blood, even in the dust." Eventually, the Spanish were defeated, and they returned home with half their ships sunk. Despite this skirmish with Spain, Elizabeth I's reign is seen as a time of peace, prosperity, exploration, and the rise of the arts.

What does the queen do after she burps?

She issues a royal pardon!

Which female fighter wins the gold medal for bravery?

Liang Hongyu was born in China over 900 years ago. The daughter of an army commander, she became an expert in fighting. She was held captive after her father died in battle, but bought her freedom and went on to become a general in her husband's army. Liang led a number of battles on the Yangtze River, and directed her soldiers by beating a drum. Enemy soldiers were frightened of her, and some ran away when they spotted her banner on the battlefield.

Whose courage is celebrated with a national holiday?

France still honors **Joan of Arc** every year on the second Sunday in May. Born around 1412, this peasant girl claimed angels and saints told her to drive the English invaders out of France. She bravely led the French army to an incredible victory over the English at Orléans. Unfortunately, Joan was captured and handed over to the English, who put her on trial and burned her at the stake. She was just 19 years old. Joan of Arc became one of the nine patron saints of France in 1920.

Which warrior queen fought back against overwhelming odds?

Rani Lakshmibai was born in 1828 in Varanasi, India. She was raised by her father, who encouraged her lessons in horseback riding, archery, shooting, fencing, and self defense. This was very unusual for the time! Rani married the Maharaja (a king) of a city called Jhansi. When her husband died, Rani was bullied by the British occupiers, who seized her possessions and ordered her to leave the palace. She refused, and gathered a rebel army. The British stormed the city, but Rani tied her son to her back, and bravely fought back using a sword in each hand. She lived and died for her country.

Did any women fight in the American Revolutionary War?
The conflict between the thirteen American colonies and Great Britain began in 1775 and lasted 8 years. When men joined the military, women usually stayed at home. Margaret Cochran Corbin decided to travel with her soldier husband, and care for the wounded. At the Battle of Fort Washington in 1776, Corbin dressed as a man and helped her husband load his cannon. When he was killed, she kept firing against the British, impressing her fellow soldiers with her aim. In the course of the battle, Corbin was seriously wounded and captured by British forces. After the war, the Continental Congress recognized her bravery. She was given a lifelong pension (half the amount given to male soldiers), and a new suit to replace the one ruined on the battlefield.

Whose heroic acts during the American Civil War have become legendary?
Harriet Tubman risked her life working as a "conductor," helping enslaved people escape to freedom in the North through a network of safe houses and secret routes called the Underground Railroad. During the war, Tubman spied on the Confederate Army and gathered information about enemy positions and where they had placed explosives. During her 19 undercover trips to the South, she escorted 300 slaves to freedom without losing a single passenger.

Whose dedication saved thousands of lives in World War I?

Elsie Inglis was born in 1864, and trained as a doctor at the Edinburgh School of Medicine for Women. At the outbreak of the First World War, Inglis was convinced that women's medical units should be allowed to operate on the front line. The War Office rejected this idea and told her: "My good lady, go home and sit still." Undeterred, Inglis raised funds and established the Scottish Women's Hospitals for Foreign Service. In all, Elsie Inglis formed 14 medical units across France, Serbia, Corsica, Thessaloniki, Romania, Russia, and Malta. One Russian government official who saw her in action commented, "No wonder England is a great country if the women are like that."

Let's take to the sea! Who was a naval pioneer?

Today, there are over 50,000 women serving in the U.S. Navy, but it all started with **Loretta Walsh**. She made history as the first woman to enlist and serve in a non-nursing role in any branch of the U.S. armed forces. In 1917, the U.S. Navy allowed women to join up, and guess what? They were paid the same as men! Both genders received a whopping $28.75 per month.

Which brave girl's words from World War II have become famous all around the world?

Anne Frank was 11 years old when Nazi Germany invaded the Netherlands in 1940. As a Jewish girl, her life changed overnight. The Nazis introduced rules that forbade Anne to visit the park or cinema. She had to enroll at a separate Jewish school, and her father lost his business. Things got worse and worse. To escape being taken away to a "labor camp," the Frank family hid in cramped secret rooms in another family's house. During the two years that Anne spent in hiding, she kept a diary where she wrote about her feelings, fears, and thoughts. On August 4th, 1944, the Franks were discovered, and Anne's family was sent to the Auschwitz concentration camp. Anne, her sister, and her mother all died there. After the war, her father, Otto, discovered his daughter's diaries. He published them in the hope that the world would learn of the horror that discrimination and racism can cause.

Which courageous woman fought back against the Nazi invasion?

Marie-Madeleine Fourcade led the largest spy ring in the French resistance. Her code name was "Hedgehog" because, according to a fellow resistance fighter, "it's a tough little animal that even a lion would hesitate to bite." Fourcade recruited spies, radio operators, pilots, and couriers, while keeping up constant communication with British intelligence in London. She was a master of disguise, often dyed her hair, and wore false teeth and thick glasses. She was captured twice by the Gestapo (the Nazi police), but managed to escape each time. Upon her death in 1989 at the age of 79, Marie-Madeleine Fourcade became the first woman to be buried at Les Invalides, the final resting place of France's most heroic figures.

Which team of amazing women changed the course of World War II?
Let's hear it for the British ladies at the headquarters of the World War II codebreaking operation in **Bletchley Park**, U.K. Seventy-five percent of the recruits there were women, and were trained to operate decoding and communications machinery. Some became code-breaking specialists. The Germans were convinced that their secret Enigma codes were unbreakable. With the help of an early computer called "The Bombe," mathematician Alan Turing and the team at Bletchley Park were able to decipher German commands and pass vital information to the Allied fleet. Meanwhile, over in the U.S., 10,000 women codebreakers were working behind the scenes to decode German communications and provide crucial information to the U.S. Army and Navy.

Which group of wartime women has been forgotten by the history books?
At the beginning of WWII, Britain was in trouble. Timber was needed to build aircraft and ships, support coal mines, and construct communication systems. There was a limited stockpile, and the male forestry workers had gone to war. Reluctantly, the British government formed the Women's Timber Corps, nicknamed the Lumberjills. These dedicated women started work at 7 AM, felling trees, operating sawmills, and loading the timber onto trucks in all weather conditions. Despite these hardships, the Women's Timber Corp recruited 15,000 women.

MOVERS AND SHAKERS

Who runs the world? Women!

Who is one of the rising stars of the political scene?

Known as "AOC," **Alexandria Ocasio-Cortez** became the youngest woman to serve as a member of the U.S. Congress at 29 years old. She was born in New York City, graduated from Boston University and, on the death of her father, worked as a bartender and waitress to support her family. Running on issues such as environmental justice, healthcare for all, and tuition-free public college, AOC pulled together a campaign for Congress in 2018. She used passionate speeches and social media campaigns to build a relationship with her voters, and, despite the odds, defeated the 10-term Democratic Congressman, and then her Republican opponent to take her seat in Congress.

UNITED STATES

Which head of state has little power, but enormous influence?

Queen Elizabeth II is Britain's longest-reigning monarch, having been on the throne for over 68 years. She holds a weekly "audience" with her Prime Minister, and has counseled 14 leaders in total during her time as Queen. Although she is supposed to remain politically neutral on all matters, the Queen "advises and warns" the Prime Minister when she feels it is necessary. Her favorite audiences were with wartime leader Winston Churchill.

Which female world leaders have achieved stand-out success?

Angela Merkel became the first female Chancellor of Germany in 2005, and in 2013 was elected to a historic third term in office. Due to her experience, she is often called "the decider" on major European issues. During her 15 years in office, Merkel has created a strong economic system, made Germany a world leader in green energy, introduced financial support for both parents after the birth of a child, and supported a law to give all workers a minimum wage.

GREAT BRITAIN

GERMANY

INDIA

Did anyone's time as a leader not go well?

On January 24, 1966, **Indira Gandhi** made history as the first female Prime Minister of India. She came from a political family, as her father, Jawaharlal Nehru, had led the campaign for India's freedom from British rule. The challenges that she faced in government included crop failures, food shortages, poverty, and student unrest. Things went downhill, and in her second term, Gandhi was assassinated by her own bodyguards as she walked to her office.

Which trailblazer was a Native American leader?

Wilma Mankiller was the first woman to serve as Principal Chief of the Cherokee Nation. She was an activist and campaigner who worked with communities to restore pride in Native heritage. Wilma founded the Cherokee Nations Community Development Department, bringing water lines to families with no running water and repairing unsafe houses. As chief of the Cherokee nation she focused on education, job training, and healthcare. In 1998 she was awarded the U.S.'s highest civilian honor, the Presidential Medal of Freedom.

Which monarch was the first (and last) queen of her country?

In 1891, Liliuokalani became the first, and only, reigning Hawaiian queen. She focused on the education of the island's children, and was a talented musician and composer. She vocally opposed the growing control of the United States government, and wanted to restore some of the power that the Hawaiian monarchy had lost. Despite Liliuokalani's bitter struggle, Hawaii was annexed by the United States.

Which fearless female leader faced up to an enormous challenge?

As President of Liberia from 2006 to 2018, Ellen Johnson Sirleaf served as the first woman elected head of state in the whole of Africa. Her challenges were enormous. Eighty percent of the population was unemployed, hunger and illiteracy were rife, and the country was crippled by enormous debt. Four years after her election, most of the debt had been erased, and she had secured millions of dollars in foreign investments. She established the right to free education, as well as equal rights for women, and built over 800 miles (1,287 km) of new roads.

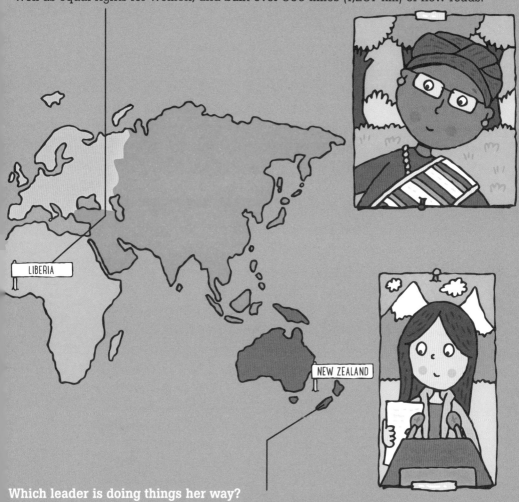

LIBERIA

NEW ZEALAND

Which leader is doing things her way?

In 2017, Jacinda Ardern became the world's youngest head of state when she was elected as New Zealand's Prime Minister at the age of 37. In 2020, under Ardern's leadership, New Zealand was one of the only countries in the world that knocked out the transmission of the COVID-19 virus. During her time in office, Ardern also promised free sanitary products to school-aged girls, planted 248 million trees, banned single-use plastic bags, outlawed semi-automatic guns, won a landslide general election . . . and gave birth to a daughter!

Whose career in politics had an unconventional start?
Born in 1928, **Shirley Temple** was a child star who sang and tap-danced her way through over 40 Hollywood films. After winning an honorary Oscar at 6 years old, Shirley retired from movie-making at the grand old age of 22! She became active in the Republican Party, and was appointed as a U.S. delegate to the United Nations in 1969. She followed that by becoming the U.S. Ambassador to Ghana in 1974, then Czechoslovakia in 1989. She was the first woman to be appointed to this position, and worked hard to establish new relations with the Czech government after the fall of the Communist regime.

Which political pioneer blazed a trail in the U.S. Congress?
Shirley Chisholm broke new ground as the first Black woman to be elected to Congress in 1968. In her seven terms in the House of Representatives, she fought hard for minority education, employment opportunities, and Vietnam veterans. In 1972, she made history once again when she became the first Black American to run for President. She launched her campaign with a powerful speech:
"I am not the candidate of Black America, although I am Black and proud. I am not the candidate of the women's movement of this country, although I am a woman and I am equally proud of that. I am the candidate of the people, and my presence before you now symbolizes a new era in American political history." Today, over 50 delegates to the U.S. Congress are women of color.

Which iconic lawmaker was a champion of justice?

From her appointment in 1993 to her death in 2020, **Ruth Bader Ginsburg** served for 27 years as a judge in America's highest court, the Supreme Court. She fought fiercely for women's equality, civil justice, disability support, and LGBTQ+ rights. Ginsburg graduated first in her class from Columbia Law School in 1959, and made her mark as a lawyer for the American Civil Liberties Union, arguing for gender equality before the Supreme Court. In 1993, President Bill Clinton appointed her to the court as a justice. She dedicated the rest of her life to the Supreme Court, and was a towering force who always stood her ground.

Which Harvard law student made history?

In 2015, U.S. President Obama appointed **Loretta Lynch** as Attorney General (the chief lawyer of the United States government). She was the first Black woman to hold that position. Lynch's father was active in the civil rights movement, and had taken his daughter to watch legal cases at their local courthouse in North Carolina as a child. This was where her sense of justice was founded. As Attorney General, her priorities included police reform, minority rights, and criminals re-entering society after serving their sentence. Her goal was to create a fair and smart justice system, which meant that those returning home from prison were given a "meaningful second chance."

GAME CHANGERS

Let's introduce ourselves to the activists and freedom fighters who helped change the world for the better!

Where do we start?

It's 1797. **Sojourner Truth** was born into slavery, bought and sold four times, and suffered violent punishment and harsh labor. In 1827, she escaped with her baby daughter, and a sympathetic family bought her freedom for $20. Truth gave lectures and speeches about the evils of slavery. Her autobiography, titled *The Narrative of Sojourner Truth*, was published in 1850, and she continued to fight for racial and gender equality. She was invited to the White House to meet Abraham Lincoln, and became active in the Freedmen's Bureau, which helped formerly enslaved people to rebuild their lives.

THE WAY TO RIGHT WRONGS IS TO TURN THE LIGHT OF TRUTH UPON THEM

Who used her writing to expose injustice?

Ida B. Wells-Barnett was an activist, journalist, and an unsung heroine of the civil rights movement. When Wells was 25, she launched and edited the Free Speech and Headlight newspaper, and was courageous in exposing the truth about the appalling crimes committed against Black communities in the southern U.S. She faced danger and hostility, and a mob destroyed her printing press in Memphis in an effort to silence her. She continued to speak up, and toured the U.S. and U.K. to shine a spotlight on the injustices faced by Black Americans.

Whose bravery and determination helped change the law?

On December 1, 1955, Rosa Parks was traveling home from work on a bus in Montgomery, Alabama. The city's buses were segregated, with Black passengers forced to ride in the back and white riders at the front. Parks refused to give up her seat when ordered to by the white bus driver. She was arrested, and so began the bus boycott. Black commuters, who made up 70% of Montgomery's bus passengers, refused to travel by bus. They shared cars, or walked miles to get to work or school. The boycott lasted a year, until the U.S. Supreme Court ruled that the bus segregation law was a violation of the Constitution. Having made history, Rosa Parks was among the first to ride on the newly integrated bus.

Which activist battled for nearly 50 years for an apology from the U.S. government?

Aiko Herzig-Yoshinaga was a second-generation Japanese American who grew up in Sacramento, California. She was 17 years old when Japan attacked Pearl Harbor, Hawaii, during WWII. Her life changed overnight. She became one of 120,000 Japanese Americans who were forced to give up their livelihoods and travel to concentration camps in the U.S. Aiko and her family were held in a dry and dusty settlement called Manzanar, where they endured primitive conditions with little privacy. In the 1980s, Herzig-Yoshinaga joined the National Council for Japanese American Redress and began to uncover evidence from WWII confirming that Japanese Americans had never been a threat to U.S. security. In 1988, an official apology was given and $20,000 was granted to each concentration camp survivor.

RECOGNIZE OUR SKILL!

How have women fought to be paid as much as men?

In the summer of 1968, 200 women workers walked out of the Ford Motor Company plant in Dagenham, London. They were skilled sewing machinists who made car seats, and were challenging unfair wages. Despite their skill, they were paid less than the men who swept the factory floor. The U.K.'s Secretary of State for Employment, Barbara Castle, backed the women, and after refusing to work in a four-week strike, the women won a pay increase. Their protest led to the Equal Pay Act of 1970, and 14 years later the machinists were finally classified as skilled labor.

Which brave activist's fight put her life in danger?

Malala Yousafzai was born in Mingora, Pakistan, in 1997. Her father ran the girls' school in her village and she loved to learn. All that changed in 2008. The Taliban extremists took over the country and banned girls from going to school. Yousafzai became a target when she spoke publicly about her right to be educated. When she was 15 years old, a gunman boarded her school bus and attempted to assassinate her. Yousafzai survived. As she recovered, she continued her fight for girls' rights, spoke at the United Nations, and, at 17 years old, was the youngest person to receive a Nobel Peace Prize. With her father, she started the Malala Fund to help girls around the world get free, safe, and good quality education.

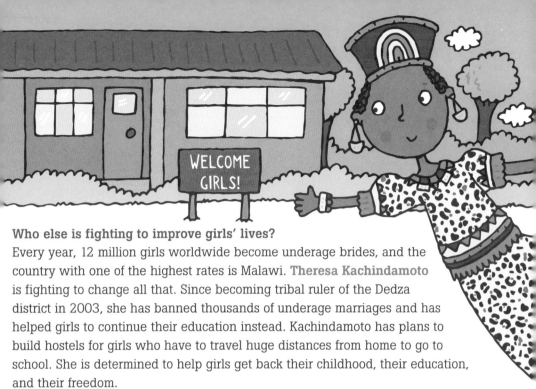

Who else is fighting to improve girls' lives?
Every year, 12 million girls worldwide become underage brides, and the country with one of the highest rates is Malawi. **Theresa Kachindamoto** is fighting to change all that. Since becoming tribal ruler of the Dedza district in 2003, she has banned thousands of underage marriages and has helped girls to continue their education instead. Kachindamoto has plans to build hostels for girls who have to travel huge distances from home to go to school. She is determined to help girls get back their childhood, their education, and their freedom.

Who is a mover and shaker for equality in Mexico?
At 11 years old, **Eufrosina Cruz Mendoza** fled her village. She learned Spanish, graduated college, and began to teach in poor communities. She returned to her home village, and ran in the mayoral election, but her application and votes were destroyed. Cruz Mendoza didn't give up. She appealed to human rights organizations and state authorities. Because of her advocacy, women's right to vote and hold office became officially protected in the Constitution of Oaxaca.

Who else has battled for her right to vote?
In the U.K., the equal rights, or suffragette, movement was founded in 1907. Women protested by chaining themselves to railings, setting fire to mailboxes, disrupting Parliament, and going on hunger strikes. Emily Davison shocked the nation when she threw herself under the king's horse in the 1913 Derby race. In the United States, members of the National Women's Party picketed the White House. To the surprise of President Wilson, the activists kept up their campaign for 16 months. Many were arrested, and the prisons began to fill with suffragettes who had to endure beatings, worm-infested food, and forced feedings.

When did the American suffragettes' campaign succeed?
On November 2, 1920, women across the U.S. voted for the first time.

Were all women in the U.S. able to vote then?
No. The vote was restricted by race, age, education, and marital status. Many Black Americans, Native Americans, and Asian Americans were excluded, and it took another 45 years and the signing of the Voting Rights Act of 1965 for the voting rights of all citizens to be equal.

Where did women first get the right to vote?
In 1893, New Zealand became the first nation to allow women to formally vote in a national election, but they still couldn't run as candidates. By 1960, half the countries of the world had granted women the right to vote, with Switzerland following in 1971, Iraq in 1980, Western Samoa in 1991, then Kuwait in 2005.

Many women fought long and hard for equal voting rights.
Who are the stand-out suffragettes?

SYLVIA PANKHURST

What was this suffragette's background?
Sylvia was the daughter of the founder of Britain's suffragette movement, but was suspended from the Union when she argued that working-class women should be equally involved in the voting rights campaign. Unlike many middle-class campaigners at the time, Sylvia was troubled by the struggles facing all women: treatment in the workplace, lack of education, food prices, poor health, and childcare.

ZITKÁLA-ŠÁ

Who did she campaign for?
Born in 1876, Zitkála was a member of the Yankton Dakota Sioux, and in 1926 founded the National Council of American Indians. The organization aimed to unite the tribes across the U.S. to gain the vote for all Native Americans. She traveled to Washington on numerous occasions to draw attention to the poor living conditions and unsatisfactory education that most Native Americans received.

SAROJINI NAIDU

What inspired this suffragette?
Indian-born Sarojini came across the suffragette movement as a 16-year-old student in Cambridge, U.K., and remained an activist and campaigner for women's rights and social welfare for the rest of her life. She became the first woman president of the Indian National Congress, and she paved the way for women's suffrage to become law under the Constitution of India in 1947.

Let's turn to the phenomenal women who campaign to protect our planet!

Who was one of the first to bring our attention to the dangers facing Earth?

Rachel Carson was born in 1907, and developed a deep interest in the natural world from a young age. She trained as a marine biologist, then became a nature writer in the 1950s. Her book *Silent Spring* alerted the world to the dangers of environmental pollution, and how chemicals used for pest and disease control were affecting the planet. Carson was convinced that the planet's ecosystem was near its breaking point. She was threatened with lawsuits from the chemical industry, but stood firm in her beliefs. Carson's writing led to the banning of a number of agricultural chemicals, and influenced government decision-making around the world.

Which environmental visionary planted trees to help solve food shortages?

In the 1970s, the women of Kenya were concerned. Their food supply was declining, streams were drying up, and they had to walk farther and farther for firewood. Wangari Maathai formed the Green Belt Movement to improve the lives and environment of these women. They were encouraged to grow seedlings and plant trees which would bind the soil, store rainwater, and provide food and firewood. In all, Wangari's organization helped to plant over 30 million trees. She was the first African woman to be awarded the Nobel Peace Prize "for her contribution to sustainable development, democracy, and peace."

Which amazing activist is known as "the Queen of Recycling"?
In **Isatou Ceesay's** village in Gambia, trash gets stored behind a family's home, as they don't have the luxury of waste collection. Plastic bags, in particular, cause a huge problem. They fill with water and attract mosquitoes, give off toxic fumes when they're burned, and become hazardous to animals and young children. Isatou figured out a way to recycle these bags by weaving them into purses, wallets, mats, balls, and jewelry. She started the Njau Recycling and Income Generation Group, a community organization that provides a livelihood to over 100 women and helps to reduce plastic waste.

Which teenager leads the worldwide fight against climate change?
In August 2018, **Greta Thunberg** began a protest in front of the Swedish parliament building, which she promised to continue until her government had reached its carbon emissions target. Just four months later, over 20,000 students had joined her campaign in countries including Australia, the U.S., Belgium, the U.K., and Japan. She has called for governments and businesses around the world to work faster in reducing carbon emissions and stop investing in oil, coal, and gas extraction. The burning of these fuels increases Earth's temperature, resulting in rising sea levels, melting ice caps, wildfires, and drought. In 2019, Greta visited New York to speak at the UN's climate conference, traveling by racing yacht to reduce the environmental impact.

EQUAL RIGHTS!

Girls around the world deserve the right to be educated, safe, and treated equally. You can help make this happen!

How can I make a difference?
Get informed! Read articles, listen to podcasts, and watch documentaries. Learn about injustices and campaigns that help girls fulfill their potential. Find out about girls' global access to education, equality, and healthcare.

What are some ways I can get involved?
Get some opinions. What are the problems that people around you would like solved?

- What would your classmates like to have changed or improved?

- Are you a good listener? Are you confident in communicating your ideas as part of a team? Think about running for school council or for a school leadership position.

- Volunteer and get involved. This will help you to gain knowledge, experience, and a network of like-minded activists.

- Be creative and have fun. Activism takes many forms, including crafting, music, cooking, and art.

- Just do it! Have the confidence to know that you deserve to be heard.

So, I've got my cause. What next?
You'll need to find fellow activists to help you with your petition, march, or digital campaign. Think about writing a slogan, or a press release for the local news. Practice a radio interview with a friend, and try to have a friendly debate when someone takes a different point of view. Always keep learning, and remain open to new information and ideas. Advocating for change has its ups and downs, so don't get discouraged if you reach a setback. You're in it for the long haul, and you can make a difference!

CHECK OUT ALL OF THE FANTASTIC FACTS IN THIS SENSATIONAL SERIES!

100 Questions about the
Amazon Rainforest

100 Questions about Bugs

100 Questions about Cats

100 Questions about Colonial America

100 Questions about Dinosaurs

100 Questions about Dogs

100 Questions about Extreme Weather

100 Questions about How Things Work

100 Questions about the Human Body

100 Questions about Oceans

100 Questions about Outer Space

100 Questions about Pirates

100 Questions about Rocks & Minerals

100 Questions about Sharks

100 Questions about Spies

100 Questions about Women Who Dared